CONTENTS

WOO HOO

READY

AIM

FIRE

UH-OH

OH-YEAH

This planner is designed to uncover your unique path, creative greatness and bring your dreams to life while living your creative flow. I have simplified this process as much as possible.

A Brief Note About Whispers

Whispers? What do I mean by whispers and playbook? Why not just call it a planner for your ideas and projects? Well, as you dive into the 5-minute quests you'll see why.

But the short answer is -- a whisper has no conclusion to what must be done with it. An idea often appears in your head along with a bunch of other thoughts. Then you try to figure out how to make it happen. There's nothing wrong with that, but this process is very different.

Whispers are about living in each moment and allowing the whispers to be revealed through curiosity, and playful exploration. Most importantly it's simple, fast, fun and creates more flow and freedom than you ever knew was possible.

Let's play!

WOO HOO

THE SIMPLE WAY

WhisperMap is based on one **simple concept** and one **simple tool**!

The simple concept: Creative flow includes everything with no fixed view points.

The simple tool: If it feels heavy, dense, or contracted; it's a lie. If it feels light, spacious, and expanded; it's true for you.

For example: Does judgment feel light or heavy? Do fixed view points feel light or heavy? Does limitation feel light or heavy? So, we know those are a lie.

Change happens when you're true to you. We often have beliefs and how-to ideas that were taught and entrained into our reality that aren't actually true.

5-Minute Wish List Quest

Set a timer for five minutes and ask the question below. Write until your timer stops. Remember this is not your goal list -- it's to open your mind to what you perceive about your future.

What do I wish for? What do I wish was different in life? What future whispers do I perceive?

5-Minute Wish List Quest

5-MINUTE 'CLARITY' QUEST

Look at your wish list and read it in reverse order.
Write your awareness of this order below.

Now view your list and ask for each item:
- Does this feel heavy? Add [H]
- Does this feel light? Add [L]

Then ask the [H] items if they still belong on this list.
If it does, leave it there and use the heart quest on the next page for these items.

5-MINUTE `CLARITY` QUEST

5-MINUTE 'HEART' QUEST

Write what it would BE like to have what you are asking for. Would it be creative, generative, healing, caring, nurturing, and expansive to have this?

5-MINUTE 'HEART' QUEST

YOUR TOP 5

Write the top 5 from your newly created wish list! These are your targets!

Circle the ones you are 100% congruent with and ready to actualize in your life.

Now, which one says, "Pick Me!" as the first one you'd like to map and bring life to?

READY

3-YEAR

1-YEAR

3-MONTH

21-DAY

DAILY

CREATING YOUR 3-YEAR TARGET

Take the item you chose from your top five and write the date three years from today.

What whispers do you perceive? What is it that you notice about that? Observe how it feels in your body, what is lit up?

If it feels light, include your loved ones (i.e. family, animals, etc.) and their desires.

If you are 'STUCK' go to UH-OH section.

Write down what comes through your body and being.

CREATING YOUR 1-YEAR TARGET

Write the date one year from today.

From your 3-year energy, what whispers do you perceive? What is it that you notice about that? Observe how it feels in your body.

Ask these questions:

Strategies
What are the strategies for growth?

Systems
What systems will be place?

Sequence
What sequential order feels light now?

Schedule
What can be added to the calendar?

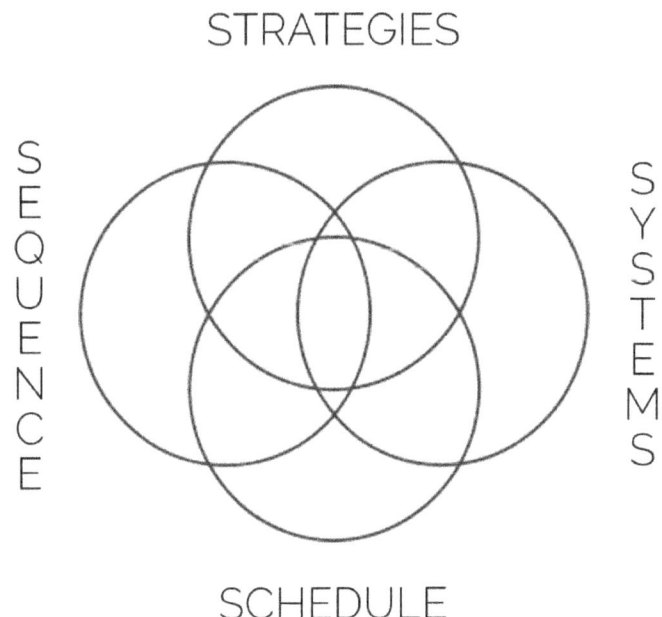

CREATING YOUR 3-MONTH TARGET

Write the date 3 months from today.

From your 1-year strategy, what whispers do you now perceive? What is it that you notice about that? Observe how it feels in your body.

Write down what comes through, then ask these questions:

Strategies
What are the strategies for growth?

Systems
What systems will be place?

Singularize or Categories
What categories or similar units may help order this creation?

Sequence
What sequential order feels light now?

Schedule
What can be added to the calendar?

CREATING YOUR 14-21 DAY TARGET

Write the date 14 - 21 days from today.

From your 3-month energy, what whispers do you perceive in the next few weeks? What is it that you notice about that? Observe how it feels in your body, what is lit up?

Start your 'Playlist' for the next 21 days and add a calendar reminder to review your playlist 14-21 days from today. You can jump to SPRINT 1: BOUNCE TIME and write this playlist on the first page if you wish.

CREATING YOUR TODAY TARGET

You will do this in the bounce section, but I didn't want you to feel lost so I'm giving you this page to offer space for that creation.

It's also important to say here, as you go forth into the AIM section that you may feel unclear or as if you did it wrong. Clients will come to me and say they're not clear, but true clarity comes when they act. Please be with this system it will offer order to the chaos you may be perceiving.

Take a breath.

AIM

AIM TRUE

In the last section I asked that you create your 'playlist' as opposed to your 'have to do' list. It's a simple shift that can change everything.

The 'have to do' list is an internal way you control creation. You make sure you do it by creating it as an obligation instead of a choice.

Being in the energy (or mindset) of choice aims you towards having your targets. If also opens the spaces to gratitude, acknowledgment and allowance.

Yes, space of being instead of doing.

For example: My aim with this Whisper System is to gift you with your natural ability to create (i.e. creative flow states.) That desire to gift you, doesn't come from I have to do this, because you have a problem. It comes from my target map question, 'What future did I come here to create?' I came here to create a different of way of functioning here on this planet.

How can you keep shifting into being when you are so conditioned to do instead of choosing and acting from being?

We have a few tools that can help with this. One of my favorites is the Be Factor (represented by a triangle). The Be Factor allows you to create from your greatness. Let me show you how it works.

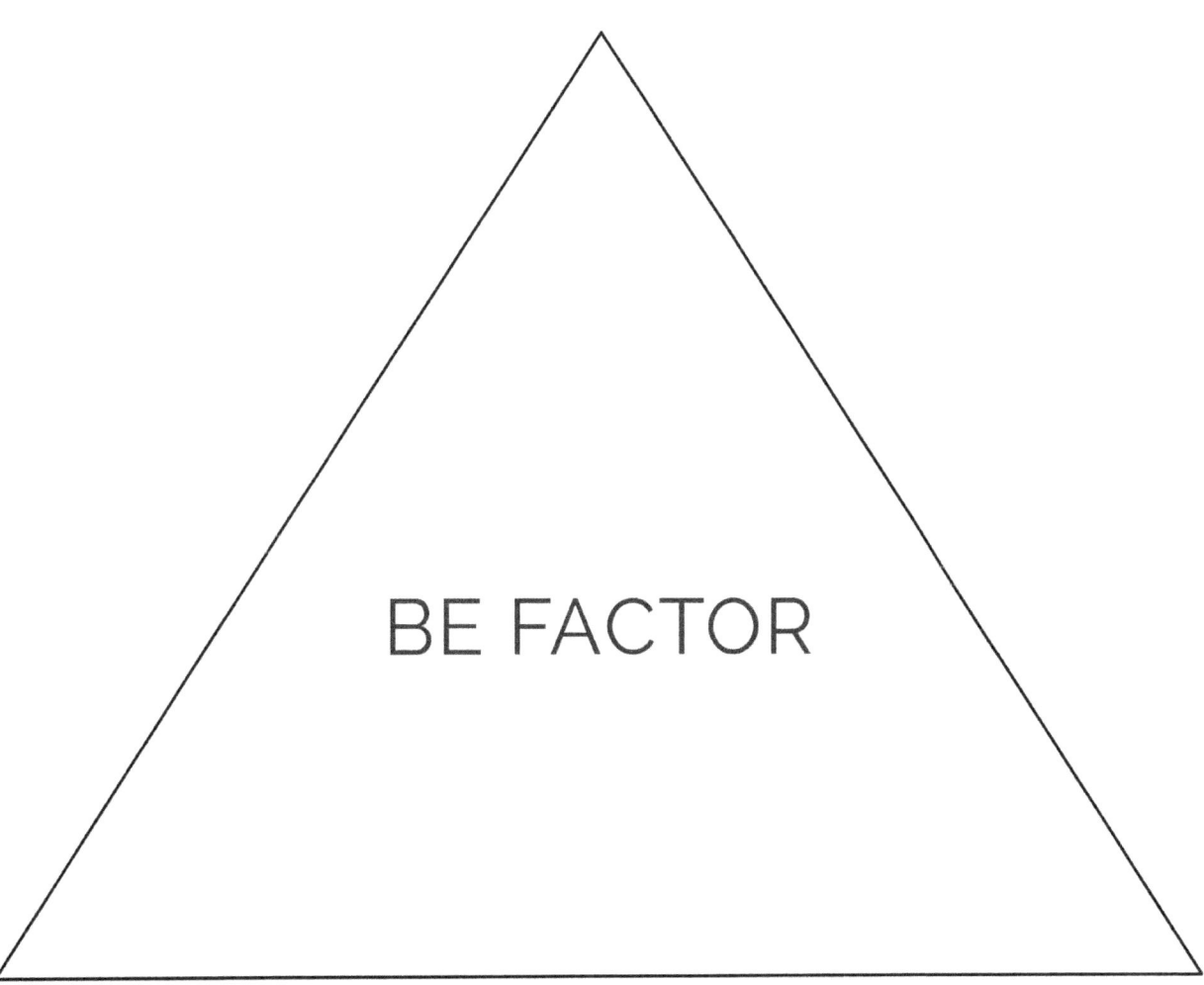

THE BE FACTOR

Imagine always choosing from your greatness, clarity and presence in each moment. I call this your BE Factor. It's the energy that you are, but sometimes don't function as. Yes! You know what I'm talking about!

You may not think of this as limitation, it's more like the idea of it's going to be hard or difficult. You can ask these questions when you simply doubt your magical capacities to receive with ease.

Here are the questions I've found that help you function as your factor of BE more of the time. The ___ is the target that may feel difficult. Example on the next page.

QUESTION 1: With ___ what am I being?

QUESTION 2: With ___ who am I being?

QUESTION 3: With ___ where am I being?

QUESTION 4: With ___ why am I being?

QUESTION 5: With ___ how am I being?

For example, if you are training for a marathon, but struggle to fit your runs in your training schedule, ask:

QUESTION 1:
With 'marathon training' what am I being? Maybe lazy or tired. Is that you truly being you?

QUESTION 2:
With 'marathon training' who am I being? Maybe my mom, dad, the teenager within. Is that you truly being you?

QUESTION 3:
With 'marathon training' where am I being? Maybe not here (or in my dorm when I was 20 years old.) Is that you truly being you?

QUESTION 4:
With 'marathon training' why am I being? Maybe I'm afraid of failure. Maybe I don't think I can do it, so I don't even try. Is that you truly being you?

QUESTION 5:
With 'marathon training' how am I being? Maybe rebellious or mechanical. Is that you truly being you?

Do you see how this offers awareness to being more of you?

FIRE

BOUNCE TIME

What if each day from the space of all possibilities you'd ask the below questions from your target map?

These question will be ask for your 14-21 day sprints and then at the end of the sprint your target will be revisted and a new playlist will be created.

I usually play for first of the month through day 21 will be my sprint, then I use the next 7 days to recalibrate.

You will see 15 bounce pages and 10 whisper pages for each month.

Use your whisper pages for new ideas, notes and things you know you may need to go back to.

KEY:
D = Desire R = Require F = Fire

D: What's my desire for today? (in regards to your target map)

D: What will I choose from my play list / what may need to be added?

D: What seems undesirable about this? Do I delegate it? Do I take it through my be factor to shift it? Do I delete it?

R: What's required?

R: What might I be resisting?

R: What might I be reacting to? (See Uh-Oh! Section)

F: What will fire me up even more?

F: What will fire this project up?

F: What stoppers can be removed to fire this up?

F: What will fire me up even more?

F: What will fire this project up?

UH-OH

DRAGON AHEAD

If you are like me, you've done your best to align and fit in with other people's ideas and points of view. You probably have a bunch of 'how-I-have-to' ideas that keep you from what's really possible.

You can come up with excuse after excuse as to why you shouldn't do this or that while denying what you really know is true for you.

Anything you defend, resist, align, react, or agree with is what I call a "dragon." These "dragons" are a great gifts as they show up to give you more awareness about what may be limiting you. However, if you don't acknowledge them you won't receive the gift and they will keep visiting you.

You can uncreate these dragons by asking them questions. Let me show you how this works.

A COMPASS FOR RECALIBRATION

The #1 tool to getting you unstuck is here! I call it the Whisper Compass. It's a continuous method of cycling through questions, whispers, and choices to gain clarity about what's light and true for you.

It starts with asking a question, perceiving the whisper and making a choice. Sometime the choice is to ask another questions.

For example:

QUESTION: "What is this sticky, frustrated feeling?"

WHISPER: That question leads to a feeling whisper. Maybe you notice that feeling had come up in the past.

CHOICE: That can lead to another question or it can lead to choice.

There is no order with this. Just flow through until you gain more clarity to what's stopping you.

See RealRawYOU.com for classes or meditations to help you with this.

5-Minute 'Course Correct'

ASK THE QUESTION(S):

- This limited feeling WHAT is this? Is it mine?

- Or something I bought from someone or something else?

- Is there something that needs to be done with it?

- Can you destroy it and let it go from my reality?

Now that you have asked more questions, dance with the Whisper Compass (whisper, question and choice) to lead back to your creative flow.

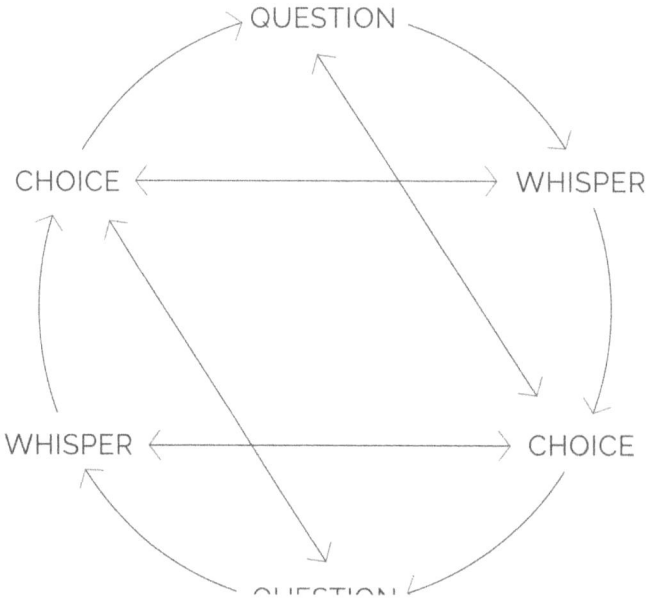

OH YEAH

OH-YEAH: FLOW

If you aren't completely absorbed with your creations you aren't in a flow state.

What if life felt like surfing the waves? What if it felt like being moved without thought -- almost as if your actions came from being?

As you play with the Whisper System you may find you will have flow moments, I invite you to allow in more of this. Visit realrawyou.com for updates.

Now, let's begin.

Sprint 1: Bounce Time

PRESS PLAY AND
BEGIN YOUR 14-21
DAY PLAYLIST

D = Desire R = Require F = Fire

D = Desire R = Require F = Fire

D = Desire R = Require F = Fire

D = Desire R = Require F = Fire

D = Desire R = Require F = Fire

D = Desire R = Require F = Fire

D = Desire R = Require F = Fire

D = Desire R = Require F = Fire

D = Desire R = Require F = Fire

D = Desire R = Require F = Fire

D = Desire R = Require F = Fire

D = Desire R = Require F = Fire

D = Desire R = Require F = Fire

D = Desire R = Require F = Fire

D = Desire R = Require F = Fire

Sprint 1: Whisper Map

BE BEST
OF WHAT EVER
YOU ARE

Sprint 2: Bounce Time

PRESS PLAY AND
BEGIN YOUR 14-21
DAY PLAYLIST

D = Desire R = Require F = Fire

D = Desire R = Require F = Fire

D = Desire R = Require F = Fire

D = Desire R = Require F = Fire

D = Desire R = Require F = Fire

D = Desire R = Require F = Fire

D = Desire R = Require F = Fire

D = Desire R = Require F = Fire

D = Desire R = Require F = Fire

D = Desire R = Require F = Fire

D = Desire R = Require F = Fire

D = Desire R = Require F = Fire

D = Desire R = Require F = Fire

D = Desire R = Require F = Fire

D = Desire R = Require F = Fire

Sprint 2: Whisper Map

Sprint 3: Bounce Time

PRESS PLAY AND
BEGIN YOUR 14-21
DAY PLAYLIST

D = Desire R = Require F = Fire

D = Desire R = Require F = Fire

D = Desire R = Require F = Fire

D = Desire R = Require F = Fire

D = Desire R = Require F = Fire

D = Desire R = Require F = Fire

D = Desire R = Require F = Fire

D = Desire R = Require F = Fire

D = Desire R = Require F = Fire

D = Desire R = Require F = Fire

D = Desire R = Require F = Fire

D = Desire R = Require F = Fire

D = Desire R = Require F = Fire

D = Desire R = Require F = Fire

D = Desire R = Require F = Fire

Sprint 3: Whisper Map

Sprint 4: Bounce Time

PRESS PLAY AND
BEGIN YOUR 14-21
DAY PLAYLIST

D = Desire R = Require F = Fire

D = Desire R = Require F = Fire

D = Desire R = Require F = Fire

D = Desire R = Require F = Fire

D = Desire R = Require F = Fire

D = Desire R = Require F = Fire

D = Desire R = Require F = Fire

D = Desire R = Require F = Fire

D = Desire R = Require F = Fire

D = Desire R = Require F = Fire

D = Desire R = Require F = Fire

D = Desire R = Require F = Fire

D = Desire R = Require F = Fire

D = Desire R = Require F = Fire

D = Desire R = Require F = Fire

Sprint 4: Whisper Map

WAKE UP
ASK QUESTIONS
BOUNCE THROUGH YOUR PLAYLIST

Sprint 5: Bounce Time

PRESS PLAY AND
BEGIN YOUR 14-21
DAY PLAYLIST

D = Desire R = Require F = Fire

D = Desire R = Require F = Fire

D = Desire R = Require F = Fire

D = Desire R = Require F = Fire

D = Desire R = Require F = Fire

D = Desire R = Require F = Fire

D = Desire R = Require F = Fire

D = Desire R = Require F = Fire

D = Desire R = Require F = Fire

D = Desire R = Require F = Fire

D = Desire R = Require F = Fire

D = Desire R = Require F = Fire

D = Desire R = Require F = Fire

D = Desire R = Require F = Fire

D = Desire R = Require F = Fire

Sprint 5: Whisper Map

WHAT GOES UP MUST
DOWN, WHAT'S YOURS IS

Sprint 6: Bounce Time

PRESS PLAY AND
BEGIN YOUR 14-21
DAY PLAYLIST

D = Desire R = Require F = Fire

D = Desire R = Require F = Fire

D = Desire R = Require F = Fire

D = Desire R = Require F = Fire

D = Desire R = Require F = Fire

D = Desire R = Require F = Fire

D = Desire R = Require F = Fire

D = Desire R = Require F = Fire

D = Desire R = Require F = Fire

D = Desire R = Require F = Fire

D = Desire R = Require F = Fire

D = Desire R = Require F = Fire

D = Desire R = Require F = Fire

D = Desire R = Require F = Fire

D = Desire R = Require F = Fire

Sprint 6: Whisper Map

YOU ARE THE WORLD

OF THE BOY

Sprint 7: Bounce Time

PRESS PLAY AND
BEGIN YOUR 14-21
DAY PLAYLIST

D = Desire R = Require F = Fire

D = Desire R = Require F = Fire

D = Desire R = Require F = Fire

D = Desire R = Require F = Fire

D = Desire R = Require F = Fire

D = Desire R = Require F = Fire

D = Desire R = Require F = Fire

D = Desire R = Require F = Fire

D = Desire R = Require F = Fire

D = Desire R = Require F = Fire

D = Desire R = Require F = Fire

D = Desire R = Require F = Fire

D = Desire R = Require F = Fire

D = Desire R = Require F = Fire

D = Desire R = Require F = Fire

Sprint 7: Whisper Map

RIDE THE LIGHTNING

Sprint 8: Bounce Time

PRESS PLAY AND
BEGIN YOUR 14-21
DAY PLAYLIST

D = Desire R = Require F = Fire

D = Desire R = Require F = Fire

D = Desire R = Require F = Fire

D = Desire R = Require F = Fire

D = Desire R = Require F = Fire

D = Desire R = Require F = Fire

D = Desire R = Require F = Fire

D = Desire R = Require F = Fire

D = Desire R = Require F = Fire

D = Desire R = Require F = Fire

D = Desire R = Require F = Fire

D = Desire R = Require F = Fire

D = Desire R = Require F = Fire

D = Desire R = Require F = Fire

D = Desire R = Require F = Fire

Sprint 8: Whisper Map

Sprint 9: Bounce Time

PRESS PLAY AND
BEGIN YOUR 14-21
DAY PLAYLIST

D = Desire R = Require F = Fire

D = Desire R = Require F = Fire

D = Desire R = Require F = Fire

D = Desire R = Require F = Fire

D = Desire R = Require F = Fire

D = Desire R = Require F = Fire

D = Desire R = Require F = Fire

D = Desire R = Require F = Fire

D = Desire R = Require F = Fire

D = Desire R = Require F = Fire

D = Desire R = Require F = Fire

D = Desire R = Require F = Fire

D = Desire R = Require F = Fire

D = Desire R = Require F = Fire

D = Desire R = Require F = Fire

Sprint 9: Whisper Map

Sprint 10: Bounce Time

PRESS PLAY AND
BEGIN YOUR 14-21
DAY PLAYLIST

D = Desire R = Require F = Fire

D = Desire R = Require F = Fire

D = Desire R = Require F = Fire

D = Desire R = Require F = Fire

D = Desire R = Require F = Fire

D = Desire R = Require F = Fire

D = Desire R = Require F = Fire

D = Desire R = Require F = Fire

D = Desire R = Require F = Fire

D = Desire R = Require F = Fire

D = Desire R = Require F = Fire

D = Desire R = Require F = Fire

D = Desire R = Require F = Fire

D = Desire R = Require F = Fire

D = Desire R = Require F = Fire

Sprint 10: Whisper Map

Sprint 11: Bounce Time

PRESS PLAY AND BEGIN YOUR 14-21 DAY PLAYLIST

D = Desire R = Require F = Fire

D = Desire R = Require F = Fire

D = Desire R = Require F = Fire

D = Desire R = Require F = Fire

D = Desire R = Require F = Fire

D = Desire R = Require F = Fire

D = Desire R = Require F = Fire

D = Desire R = Require F = Fire

D = Desire R = Require F = Fire

D = Desire R = Require F = Fire

D = Desire R = Require F = Fire

D = Desire R = Require F = Fire

D = Desire R = Require F = Fire

D = Desire R = Require F = Fire

D = Desire R = Require F = Fire

Sprint 11: Whisper Map

Sprint 12: Bounce Time

PRESS PLAY AND
BEGIN YOUR 14-21
DAY PLAYLIST

D = Desire R = Require F = Fire

D = Desire R = Require F = Fire

D = Desire R = Require F = Fire

D = Desire R = Require F = Fire

D = Desire R = Require F = Fire

D = Desire R = Require F = Fire

D = Desire R = Require F = Fire

D = Desire R = Require F = Fire

D = Desire R = Require F = Fire

D = Desire R = Require F = Fire

D = Desire R = Require F = Fire

D = Desire R = Require F = Fire

D = Desire R = Require F = Fire

D = Desire R = Require F = Fire

D = Desire   R = Require   F = Fire

Sprint 12: Whisper Map

www.ingramcontent.com/pod-product-compliance
Lightning Source LLC
Chambersburg PA
CBHW080007210526
45170CB00015B/1874